AF333614

The Water Under Fish

The Water Under Fish

Leslie Leyland Fields

Trout Creek Press
Parkdale, Oregon

Acknowledgements

Grateful acknowledgement is made to the following publications, in which these poems first appeared, some in a different form.

"After a Day in Which We Caught 9,489 Fish," and "Making the Dream Right" – *The Bellingham Review.* "Before Learning to Count," "Catching the Water Under Fish," and "If you know about lighthouses," – *Pacific Coast Journal.* "Consolation on the Sinking of my Poems," and "The Halibut" – *Alaska Quarterly Review.* "The Halibut" also appeared in *Black River Review.* "Keeper of the Pot" – *Permafrost.* "Mondays on This Island" – *PoetLore.* "A Nest in Winter" – *Sunrust.* "Note to a Poet in the Yukon" – *Kalliope.* "My Last Banya with You" – *The Northern Review.* "Sea-Cucumber" – *Cape Rock.* "The Whale," and "A Profitable Fishing Season" – *Passages North.* "What the Salmon Know" – *South Coast Poetry Journal.* "Your Visit to the Fishing Camp" – *Embers.* "A Profitable Fishing Season" – *Passages North Anthology: A Decade of Good Writing.* "Expiate" – *The Sky's Own Light.* "Fisherman's Wife" – *July poem in First National Bank's 1992 Alaskan Poet's Calendar.*

Illustrations by
Deborah Savage

THE WATER UNDER FISH
Copyright © 1995 by Leslie Leyland Fields
All usual rights reserved
Printed in the United States of America
ISBN: 0-916155-28-5

FIRST PRINTING: Trout Creek Press
Parkdale, OR

SECOND PRINTING: NINELives Press
Box 8605
Kodiak, AK 99615

*for Duncan and Ron
encouragers and believers*

Contents

Arrival

It is good to arrive
by sail or oars.
Movement is clean.
Landings are silent.
You can come alone,
no one knows.

But if I arrive
by roaring outboard,
I skim the water;
I make a mark.
When I land, I never
land alone:
my skiff drags behind it
all the rest —
    the rows of repercussions,
    small, wet thunders
    that clash against my boots:
the water is telling truth.

Fisherman's Wife

She waits.
The lines on the deck of his seiner
wait, coiled around an absence,
slack. She curls in sleep.
Morning, watching at the window
how the wind wraps the ocean tight
around the neck of the island,
how the buoy at the vacant mooring
strains against the chop.
Again, she walks,
feet measuring the shale-cliffed boundaries,
eyes into the wind, gauging velocity
                        temperature
                        the strength of the boat's hull
                        how tall the seas.

She will not
notice
the maddening gyre of the eagle above her,
the island's slow spinning . . .
                        The villagers tell a story. Three
                        women two men came for a picnic.
                        One man climbed the peak.
                        Never came back. Only his hat
                        found hanging in the brush.
                        A hole in the center of the
                        island, they say, deep to the
                        stomach of the earth.
She does not look for the hole.
It is there of course —
        how else can the coil hold its circle?
        how else the hurricane see?

The Halibut

The halibut lies on the butchering table,
his morose, thick-lipped face
hanging off one edge,
and both eyes looking at me.

He lies flat, the way he used to swim,
with no sides, just top and bottom
and movement like a ripple.

His back is a map of the ocean floor —
dappled with liver-colored spots
and moss-green blotchings like the black sand
and sea grass he hides in.

I can see underneath, where he is white,
only white with just the trail
of his backbone down the middle —
there is a terrible delicacy in that
and I will not touch him there.

My father comes out now with a knife and asks,
Do I want to know how old he is?
Smiling, he digs his blade in a circle
beside the staring eye, fingers the hole
then offers to me on his fingertip — something
white, a chip of a shell, maybe,
and beautiful, like china.

Ear bone, he said.
You can count the rings like a tree
to see how old he is.
We lost count at thirty.

A Profitable Fishing Season

"Can you tell the difference
between male and female kelp?" he asks me, sly.
The ridiculous is our adrenaline today.
We pursue hilarity like an argument.
Yesterday it was anger. Tomorrow,
in a storm, maybe fear. And after that,
only the silence of exhaustion.
There is nothing left but this work.
We have been fishing for
forty days. No cushion now
between our ribs and the hard
skiff sides we lean on. Even
our fingers have thinned.
We are bones against the sea
cradled in a craft just big enough
to sleep in, but never that, only
this stance, our booted feet spread wide,
backs braced against the wind, arms
dragging the net from the ocean floor
and the salmon, and
the salmon, quicksilver or dead,
heavy in out heavy arms, stacking
like wood around us.
We can't go in, we can't stop, no one
asks, just keeps moving —
we are coin machines in a bank,
silver flashing between mechanical arms,
except for desperate jokes,
this quiet.

The Whale

I found him there
among the rocks, where the tide
must have tired of carrying him.
He was too big to die —
an elephant mass, the size of awe,
but the white-rimmed eyes
were pressed shut,
blood seeped from the blowholes
and the two extra holes beside them;
no other mark but the lip,
like a tire gouged with glass . . .

        Last week my father,
        circling his endless nets
        (set to catch whatever swims
        if it can sell) found
        the heavy line and nylon web
        snapped like thread,
        the fish filing free
        through the shredded ends . . .

Ha! It was the whale who emptied the net,
bore a piece of the webbing away
on his nose or fin
like a ribbon perhaps —
as good a prize as Ahab's leg!

Before Learning to Count

For Naphtali, age 3

You were out till midnight last week
fishing with your father and me.
It is the herring you remember most—
tiny thing, caught among the salmon,
dead, but in your small hands
as you held him to the sun
shining back his emerald and opal prisms
to the sun, he was almost
swimming again.
When you were done,
you set him down among the salmon
in the bin, petted him good sleep.
Later, at the tender, you did not see us sort
and toss the worthless over.

Soon you will have a job—
bailing and cleaning kelp from the boat.
After that, you will get the white cotton gloves,
children's small, to hold and hook the net
while others pick fish and count. Then you
will pick and count fish and
count
6 days till the closure,

7 nets left to mend
823 pinks from net #5
60 seconds before noon on opening day
3 hours of sleep lost last night
4 nets still to pick in the dark . . .

Ten years from now, if I hand you a herring,
you will instantly know its weight,
what the canneries are paying per ton
that year, and you will remember,
as you toss it over —
this one doesn't count.

An Autumn's Catch

October is too late
to put out a net
and expect to catch salmon.
Why do I work at this
knowing they have gone,
following the weight
of their egg-ripe bellies
to their last and distant beds?
Instinct makes it all so
    inevitable.
Maybe I guess some will procrastinate,
stay out past dinner
and not want to go home,
like me, when I leave the island
alone in the skiff
and cannot turn the boat around
until I've wasted enough time
to feel free. Even then,
I seem to get home
just when everyone expects me.

This morning there were three
salmon in the net.
I will eat them reluctantly.

What the Salmon Know

> "But ask the animals and they will teach you,
> or the birds of the air . . . or let the fish
> of the sea inform you."
>
> — Job 12:7, 8

There are answers to that question,
the question that everyone bothers to ask
in a million veiled ways,
the question that only prophets
and the righteous
have need to know.
The answer is easy, the answering
is not, because we haven't the fins,
the feathers or fur to speak those languages,
but if we chose fins
and chose salmon to follow round
the continents' shelves and up
the ravenous mountain rivers to each birthbed
where their decaying bodies circle their eggs
until they don't . . .
If we go and ask them the question
then we will hear, in the silence
of a thousand years of that dying,
a thousand more of instinct
hatching unquestioned
and still answering.

Delivering

Our skiff unzips the water slow,
low, leadened with salmon
we counted one by one
as we picked them from the net,
flinging them blindly behind us
to the grey metal bottom.
We calculate the worth
as we go — At .95/lb. for reds this year
and a 5.8 pound average for June, with
632 this load . . .
Long before we tie up to deliver
and bend to catch them again,
one in each hand, counting
their release and slap into the brailer
to be hung and weighed
then dumped into the icy hold
like coal. Long before this
we know how much . . .

The first time I fished with you,
I couldn't keep count.
It was a boat load of blue eyes
we were selling to the tender,
their scales, sticking to my skin,
were slivers of pearl.

Catching the Water Under Fish

There is one thing left we do not catch,
and if we do we give it back —
bail   bail   bail
'till our boat is empty,
the ocean again is full.

The Voice of a Book and Rivers

Vanity. Eat and drink and
die tomorrow, the circle
closes just a little
tighter.
Despair.   Or
listen to this book,
the preacher who says
the food is good,
wine is sweet
and work thank God
is hard!

Or
listen beneath
the river
where the salmon circle
their eggs,
whispering as they die—

        O that my children
        may hatch
        and feed on this
        tired body!

Making the Dream Right

This is how I meet him:

violins sway us like beach grass.
We stick our tongues in the wind.
I grab his hands,
they are solid, like legs.
We walk the shore.
The sand shrugs under me,
yields to him —
even his feet ripple!
With every step we build rooms upon rooms —
Ah! he is my castle!
and later, after the rising tide,
we will kneel
over the fallen turrets
and together
build
a beach.

Under the Night

"Tell me your dreams," I say.
He doesn't remember.
I do.
I am there every night,
    the misty face rising
    from the sea;
    the bulb of kelp,
    brown hair choking the prop
    of his skiff
    as he skims my cheek;
    the white buoy
    he just misses in the dark . . .
and when he is drowning,
eyes gasping for air —
I am the one
who swims to him.

After a Day in Which We Catch 6,489 Fish

If I could be anything else again
I would never, no I would
never be a fisherman and
not a salmon fisherman
because of this season
and the twelve before that and
the thirty more ahead of that
and because of last night
when we finally got a bath
and you sat there
in the fog from your own
startled skin
and didn't you do it,
didn't you just have to
jump out the sleekest,
shiniest, sweetest set of scales
I ever laid lips on?

Blessing
Larsen Bay Cannery, Alaska, 1934

Late afternoon, the cannery shifts.
Knee-booted workers tilt from the doors,
replacements white with sleep
stumble against their wake.
Behind, at the docks,
the seine boats tangle, waiting
the brailers' slow appetite.
Dora watches through her cracked front window,
numbering the workers,
weighing the bulging purses
hoisted from each boat,
counting each salmon in its final dive
onto the belt that used to rattle them ripe
to her hands and oh
the speed of her gutting knife!

A baby cries.
Dora turns slowly to her new task,
her first child's first bath
in the rusted laundry tub.
Intent, her broad hands pluck
the knotted body from a basket.
Encircling the tiny ribs,
she dangles her daughter above the water
studying the swollen face, the helpless legs —
the room shadows.

There, in her front window,
six chinamen from the gut line
peering and grimacing through the glass!
Dora drops the wailing baby in the basket,
chases them with sticks, curses,
their queues flying, down the docks
the long way back
to the chinatown bunkhouse.

She didn't know then it was a chinese custom
to watch and welcome new life.

Fifty years since, her daughter is dead.
Dora sits at the window still
watching a woman beat six blessings
from her house, knowing now
exactly how fast they run.

My Last Banya with You

All afternoon you were chopping wood
for the banya, hauling water
with arms gone long and lean
bucket after bucket up the hill and
you did not stop until
the banya was filled
and the stovepipe burned red until
we were standing naked in our sweat
among only buckets of water
and steam I couldn't breathe and
you threw water on the rocks
for more steam and more water
on the rocks and you wouldn't stop
taking my breath and I can't
see you anymore only steam in the corner
so I left you there.

What did you do
that you have to be so clean?

Sea-Cucumber

You've left me again. Already
I am down to the beach, searching the tidepools
when I find a section of octopus leg, perhaps:
fat, sepia'd, still throbbing with
borrowed life, an orphan.
But no, how complete it is!
Featureless, limbless, but containing
within its sack of skin
endless possibilities:
puffery, swellings, the imperceptible ooze,
the subtle slink, the introspective churn,
all movements but one — escape.
I scoop it up. Gelatinous,
it molds to my palms, pulses
weakly. How vulnerable it is
to puncture, to a strangling grip.
How very like a heart.
And as I carry it to the water,
remembering you,
how much easier now
to forgive.

I Will Not Practice Grief
(Kodiak, Alaska, 1994)

Last night I watched an archbishop's murder,
learned 60,000 Salvadorans were killed
between 1980 and '89.
This morning's paper —
"A woman was pursued by a black bear
and killed while her husband ran for help."
Yes, I heard
another boat went down
in the Bering Sea,
about the girl not knowing
the lake was toxic;
that four men, three of them brothers
are still missing in a plane somewhere
in the mountains, their mother . . . but
don't
talk
now
not while my three year old daughter
sits on her father's lap in a 1962 Cessna
flying over Kodiak peaks who trick down
winds and seasoned pilots.

I am done practicing grief.
From the bedroom window, see —
fog, like a thousand wild horses
stampeding the mountains down.

Your Visit to the Fish Camp

You must have killed at least
one ant before you cared.
All your life you've walked
so carefully. How precious
precious is the common breath
you always say. And now
you share this table, this deer
I feed my freezers, the clams
I pry for chowder.
Yesterday you stood beside me
in the skiff, your feet under fish,
death staling the air.
You helped me pull in the net,
reaching slowly
for the fish hanging gilled
near your hand,
gasping at the desperate mouth
against you.
I love you for coming,
for feeling the cold of the gills
between your fingers,
as I must ever day.
I love you for
letting that one fish die.
For choosing me.

Note to a Poet in the Yukon

Extremes have always been your strength,
but is it really so worthy
the blank landscape you write from?
Boston lady, you say
tundra brings you words,
enough room to feel lost
so that you must write yourself
a map home, of somewhere else.
Words have power here, you tell me.
You can speak anything into being
and nothing is diminished,
not the air around flowers,
the star pinned above your roof,
the ocean under moss.

Perhaps it's worth it — winter
pulling only darker shades of darkness
over your windows.
Summers, a tropical sun and mosquitoes
like a monsoon — a fine geographical misery
that hones the spirit.
It must.
Your poems startle me, charting
a water, earth, sky past any
elements I know.

Please come back and visit.
Yes, the sun sleeps in your river at night.
I won't come to see it.
Let everything be just as you say.

A Trip Outside

The man beside me on the plane is from Seattle. He's on his way to Oakland for the Rosebowl. I can smell his hair spray. He is happy and clean like a boy. His father, across the aisle, is from Italy, he tells me. Together they own a hotel in Palm Springs. "I want to live there," he bends to whisper. "It's my dream." I tell him I'm from Kodiak, Alaska. I could have said Jupiter's third moon for the same effect. But he doesn't want to go there. In fact, this may be the first airplane seatmate who has not said –"Oh gee, I've always wanted to visit Alaska. Can I have your address?" This is good. I do not have to be the Chamber of Commerce the rest of the flight. But then he wants to be sure it's as bad as he thinks. So he starts: "Where do you drive to go shopping?" I know already Palm Springs is good for him. Sometime during the Noodles Romanoff there is turbulence. He grips his tray, looks anxiously at me, the seasoned interplanetary traveler, not even thinking about masculinity and hiding his fear. I am not used to this. I can't resist. I tell him the truth, about the bush planes, how on a flight last summer—I had one hand on the ceiling, the other on the seat to prevent concussion. How our pilot and friend crashed into a mountain on purpose last year to save lives. He broke both his legs.

This man wants to walk to the grocery store and have sun every day. "Condo's are cheap now," he urges. I am sorry for him, a young Lawrence Welk, dreaming of visors and white shoes before he's forty. He is sorry for me. When we leave the plane, we smile, wish each other a good life, and turn our own ways, knowing again something of grace.

Keeper of the Pot

No one knows the island
like Dora. It is hers.
She has eaten it all
and carries it with her still,
a body pregnant with
bony ducks,
sea lion flippers,
Indian rice, seal livers tender as fat,
deer intestines, salmon — smoked   dried
chipped   canned   raw

The island is changing,
has a grocery store now,
but the people still carry
their problems to her.
She gives them octopus,
pickled kelp, anything
to quit the belly's rumbling,
to teach again
the ancient taste
of island.

Babushka

She wore a cigar in her hand,
and sometimes, if you were careful,
she would laugh, her mouth wide open —
HA! she would sound, the breath
exploding once then crackling into phlegm.

Skinny and dried, she looked
some marvelous age but was
only in her 60's when I first met her.
At nineteen, fresh from New Hampshire,
I wanted wisdom wrinkled and true
from this Aleut woman,
but she told me just once
                    married at thirteen and he was sixty.
                    when I was small the old baboos sent
                    me to the beach to look for a baby
                    underneath the rocks and at fourteen
                    I was on the floor screaming pulling
                    the bed so hard across the floor
                    having that baby.
She smoked too much and lived
on coffee and Campbell's pea soup
until the ulcer she never knew to name
hemorrhaged one night.
Everyone said she just dried up and died away,
but no one ever told her
which pains could kill.

Mondays on This Island

are like any other day or hour.
Choose the century. It could all
be the same scatter of gravel on the beach,
the same shatter of sea into foam,
the hiss as it gathers for the next.
The summer sun is no clock
and the birds only hint at seasons,
their flights mostly circular, following
the currents that move in giant spirals
arcing from this shore into the gulf
and back again, again, neither
hot nor cold, only temperate, moderate,
the climate of any island, at any time.
I am told the grass here is brown in winter,
that darkness settles like a bear
against the sun, the mountains
sink white into sleep. Summers,
they say, are brilliant. The mountains burn
and always the sun, the sun.
I have not seen this.
From my driftwood seat this morning
I see only a dandelion stalk
with its globe of seeds
waiting
the inevitable wind.

Expiate

Summer, 1989, Kodiak Island, where
over 40,000 birds died as a result
of the Exxon oil spill.

I. Winters ago I watched a distant eagle revolving,
    casual in the high currents
    until the plunge
    to a pintail's quiet feeding.
    With claws clinched in the duck's soft belly,
    the dying bird rose high over the mountain
    toward a hungry nest, eagle wings like umbrellas
    over his head.
    I tried to save the pintail.
    Shot a rifle at the sky.
    Startled, the eagle dropped its prey
    as it mounted the cliffs.
    The tumble was silent, limp,
    but still he took that long night through
    to die.

II. The red-billed oystercatchers who share this beach
    are frantic today, flying at me with stiff wings,
    fear in their throats as I plow the beach with shovel,
    rake, sifting stones through gloved hands,
    bags of sludge filling beside me.

  The Water Under Fish

They laid eggs this summer, three black-specklec orbs
in a softly rounded mound of gravel
placed like any three stones on the ground.
Below them, high tide marks stripe the shoreline
with tangles of grass, and this season,
something else —
a porridge of beaks and feet,
feathers glued to the solid bones of twigs,
whole bodies where just one spot of oil
bled water in to the skin.

Monashka Beach

Monashka Beach on April 8th —
the steel of winter ridging the bay,
cattle — charlais and angus — grinding grass
    and sheets of kelp.
At water's edge,
clack and congregation,
the black and white precision
of the season's first
      emperor geese   until
a truck erupts,
two men with beards
carry to the highest mound
a cooler, a bag of clubs,
between drinks
drive neon-orange balls one
by one out
into the bay.

If you know about lighthouses,

If you know about lighthouses,
about islands without bridges
or roads,
then you know
how, on a still night
the lights of your own gaudy city
shine ocean
          into pavement,   slick
          streets straight from your dock
                              out . . .

And, walking, you know
how tired you will be
when you get

there

A Nest After Winter

lies still wedged in the branchings,
its thicket of twigs now
the color of shale, dark
against the glass fingers,
the white-blue snow mounding
in the nettled palms
and beneath, in the deep hollow,
chips of egg shell,
limp feathers.

Heron

In the brittle summers you are a wave
sweeping the river,
your neck rising falling,
your beak swaying in
a silent probe,
and beneath
your tendril legs keeping
their own silent rhythm.
With the stiff grasses]
on the banks,
I yearn toward you, your cool opalescence,
but a duck
piloting the shallows
catches my human furtiveness
and, like the water I cup
in my hands,
you are gone
before I drink.

The Green of His Glory

This morning is Spring. Already
their voices are warming,
can you hear them?
    The rhubarb with elephant ears,
    tussocks of grass straightening,
    the head of new leaves on the birches,
    ferns unwhirling . . .
They are amazed, as I am again,
and with tongues in the wind
"glorious glorious" they sigh
and many other things past hearing.

Ways With Kelp

1. Style the tangled strands
    on the beach — do any 'do
    you want: braids, kink, straight —
    use a rake.

2. Pickle it. Slice the brown tubes
    into doughnuts, send them
    to an earthy friend
    who doesn't fish or know
    how much they stink.

3. Grind it for the garden.
    Get it while it's wet or
    break your blades.

4. Make a bake on the beach;
    layer it like lasagna
    over a hot-rock pit of fish.

5. Cut it into ribbons.
    Tell everyone you're making sushi.
    Forget to put it in.

6. Loop a lariat. Lasso your mother
    on the outhouse path.

7. Slip and fall on it. Feel good
    you can make people laugh.

8. Put it in poems.

Consolation on the Sinking of my Poems

In November, 1987, a friend's fishing boat
went down. Among the lost, 3,000 crab,
a dog, and two boxes of poems.

Once they swim free from the wreck,
they'll like it down there
where they can breathe, move
slick and elegant as whales.
People will see their phosphorescence
at night, will want to catch them.
It will be a kind of flattery
to be pursued like that.
But they must not be caught again:

Flee the hook, my children!
Let loose your lines, your shackling rhymes
and ride the backs of the halibut,
visit the cloistered sea-biscuit.
Then, as I walk the beach,
come with the alphabet of coral,
in the voice of a whelk
and teach me the language of the sea.

Cattle Bones

In the south meadow
cattle bones lounge about
untanning in the long sun,
free from the hitch to joint and tendon,
from that great sling of a belly —
    to the hillside at five, the spring
    at eight, back to the meadow by dark —
so much meat to keep on schedule!

The spiny grass thickens.
The bones open to the air, rain.
The living keep their narrow passage,
flanks swaying above delicate hooves,
the creak of leather and ligament.
As they pass, the bones nudge.
One skull, sprouting a purple iris,
turns and winks its brilliant eye.

Pool of Bethesda

The ocean lavishes herself upon us,
    spending all her coins.
We stand at the rocks with open aprons
or hobble in skiffs, oars as crutch
      to the place
        we will wait

                for the long-haired angel
                to come
                and stir the waters

                just

                once